Sphinx

Sphinx

Cat Woodward

This collection copyright © 2017 by Cat Woodward

All rights reserved. No part of this publication may be reproduced, stored in a retrieval system, rebound or transmitted in any form or by any means, electronic, mechanical, photocopying, recording or otherwise, without the prior written permission of the author and publisher. This book is sold subject to the condition that it shall not by way of trade or otherwise be lent, resold, hired out or otherwise circulated without the publisher's prior consent in any form of binding or cover other than that in which it is published.

I Have Seen This Before I, II, III and IV were previously published in *The Literateur*; *Afterlife of Children*, *This Spring I'm Doing a Fire Party* and *Dream of House Boat with Solitude and Wicker Chair* in *Tears in the Fence*; *Sphinx* in *Visual Verse*; *The Goddess of Mercy Addresses the Fox* in *The Interpreter's House*; *The Star or Guidance* and *Hegemony* in *Brittle Star*; *Border State or Through a Glass Darkly* in *Ink, Sweat & Tears*; *Reply to Richard* in *Lighthouse*

ISBN number: 978-0-9933508-7-0

Printed and Bound by 4Edge

Cover design by Marco Guerrero
(www.altairartsmty.com)

Typeset by Sophie Essex

Published by:
Salò Press
85 Gertrude Road
Norwich
UK

editorsalopress@gmail.com
www.salopress.weebly.com

Table of Contents

I Have Seen This Before *I*	1
I Have Seen This Before *II*	2
I Have Seen This Before *III*	3
I Have Seen This Before *VI*	4
Hot Damn	5
Sayonara Suckers	6
Afterlife of Children	7
This Spring I'm Doing a Fire Party	8
Dream of Houseboat with Solitude and Wicker Chair	9
The Star *or* Guidance and Hegemony	10
Let Me Tell You How Much I Have Come to Hate You Since I Began to Live	11
It Would Not Equal One One-billionth of the Hate I Feel for Humans	12
To Hell With You	13
Sphinx	14
Trees Go Quiet	15
Mother in Garden: a portrait	16
Florence, Are Your Feelings Reasonable	17
On Looking for One's Enemy and Finding Her	18
I'm Making Iced-tea for the Very First Time	19
The Goddess of Mercy Addresses the Fox	20
Planets Suite	21
Cycle Song	32
Woods of England and Their Species	33
Border State *Or* Through a Glass Darkly	34
I Love the Moon	35
Reply to Richard	36
On the Dawning of the Age of Aquarius	37
Tender	38

I Have Seen This Before *I*

Question: Where were you born? in protest I was hopeful and packed with greenery soft as a salmon egg on the 104th day a voice came to me and said don't trust the voice that says it's with love and then I did not When were you born? when the fishes packed the sea and the lion ate of them when the windmills turned upon the earth all merrily but that question is not my business to know now is it? on the 351st day a voice came to me and said I am with love Why won't you tell the truth? if you heard it you would surely die the future's bright it's a forest fire

I Have Seen This Before *II*

Big black silence secretive as a mushroom and enormous as a state silence is the shape of an expanded chest and is a reply to nothing and it does not do these are the things I fantasise about at night sleeping diagonally I should like to be a big black silence to reply to nothing and not do I should like to be silence big and black the future's bright it's a supernova whispering pines wash up a thought of water lap a cry of bird which is both a knowing and being between one place and another tableau if you can stand a word like that or rather chorus of eyes suddenly open under an umbrella in the freshly rained fen a crow three times and sun blast through the dew-drop alive it is and thinking all the corn here breathing in the way of corn all the mirage ghost sails of boat and the silver-leaved willows all the o o o don't let it drop don't swap the swallows dry heat red-cheeked this is this is a wild raspberry sourly bleeding and a certain snake by the twitching of grasses and the grey light of its loud dry passing it pays out and out like a misheard word it could go with a choke hard falling as if from a dream of the street on which a child you lived on which a child a child you lived the fence posts are all broken and I'm scared of the neighbours' boys and girl their faces so dirty and their black eyes with such a poor poor evil light

I Have Seen This Before *III*

I hacked up a word it was 'unprogressive' I hacked up a long word it was 'drown-the-loved-ones-in-a-dark-skinned-sea' the word I hacked was 'linguistic-violence' I hacked up nothing but quote marks they clung to the ceiling like flies I am the lady of flies the fly-lover which means loved-one-hater crush a fly beneath your clean pink thumb crush the violence and love love you can die of the dry heaves you can die of maggots you can die under a clean pink thumb the greatest evil believes it does the greatest good am I an evil child? I am the enemy of all that is good in this world I hate the peace that is and the peace that will be I am the enemy of love my words are cruel and unnecessary I am not a kind person I lie and I lie to end all that is good in this world I hurt everyone especially those who do no harm I will hurt you because I do harm I am queen of lies and the Ruin is what I mean actually I feel shrivelled as a dead root all things having been misdirected I am aware that I am a fat root all things having been misdirected I must be a sick root all things misdirecting should I sorrow? o o o

I Have Seen This Before *IV*

Conservative politics is just indirect love and that is why it burns as if suffering were a specific noun in someone else's language as if compassion were auto-guilt comfort-shame I shout and cannot breathe in again I shout consciousness washes up on the shore of a red-legged bird and in her brayed ugliness-song I am a me there hearing such grey-feathered red-legged goddesses the many such waters of many-ness surfacing for a while bird-like and singing a song to someone there on the shore the future is full of invisible light the future is bright so bright so very bright I cannot see it

Hot Damn

toe on the carpet looks like a bean blood is more red from the head strawberry jam/cherry pie dogs will eat anything No means yes, no? Crowning the ring of muscle But it doesn't fit back on Girls scream like gulls What can you do when the world gets on top of you? You can be crushed And one just holding a leopard on a chain His teeth smacked the ice one incisor shooting left the other right What can you do when the world gets on top? You can be still as an oyster and as quiet No Yes mother with a small hill of pink in her hand Kids cry just like dogs have you seen *The Road*? Dogs will eat anything What can you do? You can lie back and think of America cornbread grits a bowl of raw liver beans But it doesn't go back on Elbow pulled open like a chicken wing hard ground/moped If it's not taken it's not given Falling is English for 'catch me' sometimes it's just falling A rope burn healing and other burns custard KY What can you do? You can enjoy it Hurt me just don't damage me crowning the muscle Brother forgive, yes? It's not been loved if it's not broken It's not been owned Coffee-coloured rings/jam stains dogs are the most yolo animal This is what it is A gull in mid-air tips arched fire-engine legs spread putting on the brakes Falling Falling yes yes yes Hot damn!

Sayonara Suckers

pigeon chest like a child's salt dough ash tray There's
more hair on her pubic mound than on her head thighs
like bacon but she doesn't turn you on He said veal is
force fed baby cow there's nutrition enough under your
nails for a week Her father died i was like 'ok' a dead cat
now a bag full of insects and one frog Crawling is holy
on the worms of our bellies dog shit lined the street as
though it were palm trees Take this pain away o God-
dess take this pain far away There wasn't much to say
about his skinny arms the crushed hand in which one
terminated like a dead spider in shape colour and size
In the name of wind and rain O Goddess take away this
pain i walked blackbirds impenetrable eyes soulless onion
A boy's body about 12 she lifted her dress i said 'cool'
lips like live animals he could be famous i remember the
dog vomited up something of unbearable significance
But she doesn't turn you on we have been sober through-
out all this really A white candle burning to represent
health and the moon my name on paper blood mixed
with milk lemon verbena string The canned herring whose
eyes blazed with emptiness and venom brother's bronchial
thunder calling for interim cloud In the name of wind and
rain Her pagan eyes like disused bathrooms like cephalopods
O Goddess take away this pain in the name of wind and rain

Afterlife of Children

now that you're here in the afterlife of children
you are a penny at the bottom of the well
of yourself

and the Ode to Joy is playing

this is a happy time
so happy that you're crying tears
the shape of little cartoon skulls

This Spring I'm Doing a Fire Party

Tristan in the car
Tristan not in the car

and that other thing
like men singing

Michael by the river
Michael on the river

next to me

to love boys
like green and yellow

boys

Dream of Houseboat with Solitude and Wicker Chair

think about the opposite of job
that is
think about cats

and think about the opposite of married
which is bowls
of many-coloured candies

this is the tantrum i am having
lush and live as plants

The Star *or* Guidance and Hegemony

no moth no spider   no wild flowers no pouring of water upon the dirt   no beer can   no building   no shadow that scours   no blackbirds   no belly   no stripe of sun   no crying   crying is not true   no toil no onions   no cat skull inhabited by snails   no habitation no cat no snails   no omens no women no wheelchair   no emergency emergencies are not true   no emerald no genitals   no surprises   no killing of wolves no punching of bears   no shouting no echo   no drunkenness no hangover no wine no gap year no crossing the palm   no sallow breast no dropped arm no alarm clock   no dragon king no scaly hides no devil no tower   no camping no kneeling on the grass no self-abuse   no milk-tooth no baby-bone no baby   no mephedrone no past where my mouth should be   no nakedness   naked is not true   no body that desolates as I in turn was desolated   no barking   no biting   no crying no phallic imagery   no poetry   poetry is not true   no cyborg   no garden   no hopelessness   no ever-flowing source no driving stream   no wild flowers no pouring of water upon the dirt   no running   no job   no sadness   no crying   no crying

Let Me Tell You How Much I Have Come to Hate You Since I Began to Live

as the fragrance from the flower
as the crow atop the corn stalk
forever

you are my lambchop
my bunny
you are

even when you are not

stand there
where I can see you
and, as if you were dying,
die

It Would Not Equal One One-billionth of the Hate I Feel for Humans

a chest is a place to sit
and there and there

the unbroken summer thunder
of it

proud it is
and true

and bigger
and louder

than that other thing

whatever
it is

To Hell With You

I would not
wish happiness
on any of you

not

on your pulped face
like a brown apple

not

on the worm in it

it's just
the principle
of the thing

not personal

understand this
because
you must

Sphinx

are you speaking with my mouth? are you speaking with my dirty mouth? sliding into me at a painful and necessary intersection, this is how we occupy the same point in space: i will kill you. not so recombinant but enduring community, when a boy who is a girl, a sphinxing boy, is always slipping off the eyeball, such a womanly blue boy and with redder hair like a dirty-talking sunset. like her i am picturesque isolationist terrorism. riddle me that. over here persons are lambent as anemones, persons sway in the dark stir of the sea erotically, light dark persons and we say abide with me. in your fairness and my stupidness abide, in that yellow dress, in that hateful shirt abide, abide in your working and in my not working, in your all-levelling colourlessness (and in mine) abide, lie and when you do so abide. there is a moistureless desert which abides, there is a petrified wood which abides, in them are houses suddenly abandoned, the planets pass over them and abide. summers of biding and abiding, for in the winter we die. so if to say cedar is to smell cedar, then what am i? if a bird is a snake and a lion is a girl then get your eye off my eye! keep that mouth away from me! you wear a face of quietly sad dislocation because you do and i am off-broken, drifting above vague, gloaming anemones because i am. when the voice that ends me calls it calls like i do, traumatised, needy, righteous and raging. the sphinx is the beast of peace i sent to devour you, with just your head left, sticking out.

Trees Go Quiet

The trees go quiet
    as a sunrise of pure underwhelm
    and strictly lapine homesickness
    is us ghosts without spirit animals.
    if it is earthliness then i will be the
    worm, will do Being, brutely. in this
    fatherly land, is Dandelion-death-
    of-the-daffodil, unheard below the
    dead horses, flogged. we have
    5000 flavour combinations.

The trees go quiet
    and the honeyed hexagram, sucked.
    fed to death on nothing at all, i am
    loamly and forgetting, dumping all
    my fear in the sea. nothing but your
    loveliness wear, and night is all things
    but one, sleeping. this gift is a golden
    goose, yielding, mathematical, this
    gift is fatly accessible and very axed.
    but i don't want that gift.

The trees go quiet
    when nothing gives but the ice and
    could, if there were time, go on like
    this forever. we, the object of our
    consumption, lovesick for both the
    bumblebee and the whale. we, with
    a love who hoes in his pain. moon-
    mad for inconvenience, like a bitter
    herb for a woodland spirit. blackbird
    sings 'silly you, silly you, so true.'

Mother in Garden: a portrait

impersonal flourish of cells
and over there the hibiscus

all so where

when you get the void that binds
or love

such as in this poem:

the flower extends the arm
that the flower is not the arm

and the set of all petals
is not itself a petal

Mother, be weather
be stickle brick, picture

so where
and with love

all being in the air
like radio, like rain

Florence, Are Your Feelings Reasonable

Florence, are you having enough fun today
Florence, are you the right kind of busy
who do you hate, Florence
are you disquietude
by a muddy river
eating very cheap sandwiches?

On Looking for One's Enemy and Finding Her

i eat. i eat her
dog her. dog eats
me she. i eat myself. i
dog eat dog. eating girls
dog me. me eat. i would like to
meet someone. a girl who likes dogs.

*

spaghetti with pork sausages.
shake can. hiss like.
spaghetti with pork sausages.
muttley. google how to make.
spaghetti with pork sausages.
haha.
red sauce with pig dog.
hot pig spaghetti.

*

haha. o me.
eating.
o hungry for.
eating.
o me. haha

*

constructing a sort of doorway that cannot be passed through
constructing a sort of doorway that will not be passed through
robotic dogs
where in the non-atmosphere
in the reddish liquid
help sounds like woof.

I'm Making Iced-tea for the Very First Time

only write summer poems
and speak
the way grown men speak
to a kitten

The Goddess of Mercy Addresses the Fox

he lies by my river and thinks himself a loveless little lung.
the colour is red. his face halved. blood drops in snow.

he turns over my dirt as if there were things to find.
black are his hands. his lips are pointed. i have no shame.

he is whining for a vixen.
i am not a vixen. i am quiet. my eye is green.

he cries his cry. 'nobody clips my claws'. 'nobody hears me roar'.
his mouth does not form me. i am there, pinkly glowing.

he eats my animals, and hopes as long as he's eating.
warm is my skin. a pleasure like kindness. i let the fox in.

he is dreaming of a darkness who is not my name.
i dream the fox. my hair is long. i am never alone.

in the desert there's a tree on fire and i touch him.
in my hand there's a fox and i touch him.

i cover the eyes and whisper to the ear
its name

i am singing.

Planets Suite

planet green

The planet consists primarily of a long ride down a short road to the house in a field. In the house there is a sister and a man. I have a small wooden amulet and in it the ghost of Frederick Barbarossa. The verges are a hiding and in it monsters and men dressed as monsters. One does not look behind. Dark-blind I rode my bike into a hole and stopped.

planet black

Planet black feels disquietingly familiar, as if visited when very young. The atoms, long since broken down into baser unusable elements, are now pure sound. The planet is only a vast darkness with an ash-like consistency and the music, constant, of a crowd cheering.

planet day-glo

The day-glo planet has nipples like our sky has birds, the colours inverted by an as yet undetermined law into Vogue-grayscale and thickly painted fluorescents. I am experiencing a never-before need for bodies, including my own. The indigenous dance naked for their language, they are a very politic people; blue lips, rhythmised pleasures, skin and justice. A male moves his hips up and then down, the way a female would.

planet Cassandra

Each pebble and leaf and internal organ is inscribed with a true account of the history of humanity. Every surface crammed, tiny and near inscrutable as names on grains of rice, only lapped-over until the gaps between letters become like stars in space. It's all there, all of us, everything, what was and what will be - exactly. It is a truly remarkable coincidence, but of course, just someone else's opinion.

planet yellow

Re-enact the burning in your pilgrim's clothes. Re-enact. The burning. In the specially built room. Walls of wood with nothing outside them. Room planets. A great great many of them. Outside them nothing and in them burning. Yellow and plasmic. Re-enact re-enact. Put on your best hat. But spare the cat.

planet pink

Planet pink has only weather; fleshless rains the colour of raspberries raineth every day. A pink wind makes fingers of rock and nothing feels it or knows. We see from the air looking back on the land. We do not go there. We do not morning its sunrise. We do not clamour its dumbness. It is warm and it is cold. Planet pink, planet pink, p-.

planets

Picture the milky way. But instead of stars it's planets. Like dust-motes rotating slowly. All of them (if you squint) are slightly ovoid and mildly blue, and all of them are Earth.

christmas planet

It is possessed by unthinkable timelapse. Aeons pass over it and it winks like a christmas light, with sudden periods of complete darkness. Wink in. Wink out. One desires to reach out an arm and stay the unthinkable. Such is jealous gravity and its cradling divisions of time. A transmission constantly emits a string of names.

dynasty planet

The first intelligent race to dominate the planet were the Arachnids. After the remains of these had calcified and returned to the dust came the Parrot People, whose succession was challenged and eventually compromised by the Pitcher Plant Beings. Then came the Sentient Gases, then the Constructs, then the Plasmas. It is currently the seat of the Lemur People, who (like all those before them) wage their wars from the backs of women, whose hips are mid-way birthing and whose knuckley hands knead bread.

planet silver

Upsidedown snow, hello. Lung-tooth, tears on hiatus where it's birches all round and the sky forever lavender. Hi, I remember you, with the silent sound of style. Birches dark like arrested rain and limbed as whitely as the way we paint ladies. Nothing but birches in snow, hello. Upsidedown birds in upsidedown birches, 'here!' they sing, but what was the question?

Cycle Song

fine rain falls like conscience, the colour of agate
birds' joyful cursing
parsley, sage, sorrel and bay
discloses
exact size and weight of a human hand
left of frame a black cat squatting
crow-shaped
like the moving cloud, its bull heart
like the snail's slow pace toward the sparrow
mint, rosemary
a name said three times in a mirror
the river is a rumour
out there in its square bracket

fine rain is aggregate and the colour of snails
a crow joyfully scratching
centre frame is clouds' slow pace
and black
the weight of a human heart
thyme-shaped a rumour mirrors more than
the river
birds closing
around a bullish name
conscious hand and little cat
suggest cursing, sorrowful music
face bracketed
by parsley, sage, rosemary

a gregarious rain of fine colours
the shape of sage
framed as a mirror the river
with bird joy black and wonderful
slow crow heart
like cloud, like parsley, like conscience
the weight of rumour
Morrigan cursing
a mist of exact, human names
its sorry music, rosemary and thyme
slow pace toward
bright green
the simulation ends.

Woods of England and Their Species

such dark green pinescent
such dead leaves
such sweet and rain

that when i sit up
a foot presses me
down again

tenderly and soft
because it needn't
use all its strength

Border State *Or* Through a Glass Darkly

in the black space
is the black face

of a slim black boy or girl

slender black chest
pout of lips

a round that might be a testicle
black as a plum

there are no eyelashes
there are crows that scatter but do not fly away
it is hard to tell in the dark

there is the black sound of the sea
its black-tipped waves

the sound of the deep black sea
its reach like the shadows of pine trees

the iced black of the sea
its smash of black-sequinned human fish

the blackened ankles are like knots in a rope

'Sweet Jesus,' we say
'cover me over'

I Love the Moon

the moon rises over a tree with a robot's muteness one part gutspill two parts mind your god damn business her agelessness has a particularly social silence just as fashion models do as without context as a lizard saying o a tentacle o this place of horny crustaceans and even madder dogs listen she's smoking these femme fatales are always smoking when they say things how do you think it feels to rise each night covered in somebody else's sorrow male and female sorrow sorry how am i supposed to know what the nightingale says something about where he buys rice something about noodles and a man called Will i can't pretend i'm more than the sum of my holes and what one might condescend to fill them with what one might build up an irreversible complex around what one writes a poem or a novel about the moon has something of an institutionalised relationship with the sun at this moment the sun is breathing into the moon's mouth and saying open your lips you idiot and the moon is just now learning the miracle of love she has just now become strong enough for love this is actually the most to have happened to her massive body since just after the beginning and it hurts o it hurts she is crying with her mouth full of sun and her ass full of dollars from the ground it looks as if she is crying either because she has finally released herself to the real deal called love or because her ass is full of dollars or maybe because she remembers the dream she keeps having where her dead grandmother appears only she's been there a long time with that look on her yellow face as if she were dreaming too but unlike the dreamer would never wake up the moon says hey you you have to leave me alone remember you're dead and so the moon takes her by the hand with a decisive action although she doesn't know where she is supposed to take her and then she feels especially sad because after so many years the hands of grandmothers strangled to death by psychologically unstable grandfathers feel just the same as the hands of everybody else's dead grandmother the moon is a dry river she is airless and pale and far after all she is the moon

Reply to Richard

When you take your pill
It's like a mine disaster
I think of all the people
Lost inside of you

Richard Brautigan,
The Pill versus The Springhill Mine Disaster (1968)

Mine - neither a place nor object but the negativity measured by what one can take out of it: God great patrionimbus did bless us with this provision for all things are not but gifted I feel a scouring this here pit is a maker of men we hear not ourselves but the noise of sons and fathers shouting are you stupid now as well as a whore? we knew then having no sound only echoes and daughter a silence carried on by other means spit-slung face-red filled like a pie too drunk this time to fuck me on business or I too ugly so what little myling haunts you now what snot puddle in want of a human face for all your pleasure? I didn't think so even out-side closes like a room so heavy am I and massless you'll know us only by all who came after like a shadow not even my name remaining in crowded or sparse times the rabbit will absorb a foetus back into her body at night the lotus closes God withholding nothing from his chosen ovum yolk grain cipher all those nothings inside her add up to more than her math was not her strong suit we no here no kick and scream which is the one against zeros the one that is zero the zero that is one was always the language of our people the girls and women are everywhere dying quite literally blood-knot pig-licked and ugly our people are good people and lovers of life Fuck your Devil's Doorbell Richard baby there's a big difference between lost and ontologically impossible to find Fuck your meta-sopho-pseud-biology Richard baby there's a big difference between a dead fellow and a cell fallow Fuck your matron sacrificial selfless Richard the avarice of the mining industry is nothing like my need to *be* Fuck your buried souls as if I was not a soul enough already Richard did your mother teach you nothing? for I was less than ten when I did an evil thing for I was then a woman living for I myself am not a tragedy for it has no colour and is me for it and I am also letter O when I hold on my tongue at last the word for 'no'

On the Dawning of the Age of Aquarius

That point where history and then the known world is re-comprehended in another thought-form is the greatest terror to grip us in the night since the hammer of narrative pummelled the soul with neither invitation nor remorse. It is not an irresistible and therefore un-American coercion but a synchronicity almost wholly not unpleasant, in other words, atavism, or any number of inverted pyramids. To say what you see: a practice akin to dreaming, which is the obsessive desire for dreams. We know that the particular yearning of the ear is ontologically insupportable by the aural (religious) capacity and studies show that this desire of desires is almost identical to the proprioceptual experience of dancing, that is, being unaware one's movement only to find that one is not dancing at all but sobbing or vomiting. We should ask what Freud would make of this. Regard the current trend for carbon-based simian life. Of course, it is possible to engage in two or more conversations at once or to channel remotely the voice of another, it is ostensibly a matter of slippage. Also, that happiness enters the hole of the gut through the same prehensile orifice as the fear that the subject might be at once entered and not entered leaving her standing cutely and alone(ish) on the chilliest rim of time. Specifically, it is the pillow-shaped space in which death or god suddenly arrives in one's chest with a destroying happiness, an experience shared by certain unique individuals among penguin colonies. This is how the object is considered, as subject to the greater waveform and carrying the angelic (fetishized) archetype out into space. Neptune enters the ninth house, therefore one would be a Virgo and an alcoholic. Consider, the windy Sunday sky as a bowl of light and air, or the impression of skirts rustling high above, of something that passes and does not look back, fundamentally, with a bereftness only achievable in the most extreme forms of peace. It is worth noting at this stage, humans who are shocked by the discovery that their existence is insignificant, we do not like these humans, we do not identify with this version of humanity. After all, what is the meaning of the stuffed pterodactyl hanging in the museum come hotel come business park of your unconscious fantasies? Always an interesting and difficult question.

Tender

there is this hoof in him
a kind of homelessness
made out of parties
be a largeness
be a saying hello
you are here

these are not my colours of wanting
this is me as a nanobot
as savaged seashell
i am an Easter Island head
and the cold black stars
who love that head

O
the Trinidad to his Tobago
an instruction guide in obtainable sobbing
and sudden frightening levitation

O
restless coalescence
the provisional deconstructing
of a thousand
translucent watermelons

how gentle is the finger to the poem
how closed the caterpillar to the palm